PHILADELPHIA
PHILLIES

by Dave Jackson

SportsZone
An Imprint of Abdo Publishing
www.abdopublishing.com

www.abdopublishing.com

Published by Abdo Publishing, a division of ABDO, PO Box 398166, Minneapolis, Minnesota 55439. Copyright © 2015 by Abdo Consulting Group, Inc. International copyrights reserved in all countries. No part of this book may be reproduced in any form without written permission from the publisher. SportsZone™ is a trademark and logo of Abdo Publishing.

Printed in the United States of America, North Mankato, Minnesota
052014
092014

Editor: Matt Tustison
Copy Editor: Nicholas Cafarelli
Interior Design and Production: Carol Castro
Cover Design: Craig Hinton

Photo Credits: Tom Gannam/AP Images, cover; Photo by Ronald C. Modra/ Sports Imagery/Getty Images, title; David J. Phillip/AP Images, 4, 7, 8, 43 (bottom); Rogers Photo Archive/Getty Images, 10, 14, 42 (top); Mark Rucker/ Transcendental Graphics/Getty Images, 13; File/AP Images, 16, 42 (middle); AP Images, 19, 20, 31, 34; Tony Tomsic/Getty Images, 22, 42 (bottom); Photo by Focus on Sport/Getty Images, 25, 27, 28, 43 (top); Ed Reinke/AP Images, 33, 43 (middle); Ed Betz/AP Images, 37; Dick Druckman/AP Images, 38; Rob Carr/AP Images, 40; George Gojkovich/Getty Images, 44; Matt Slocum/AP Images, 47

Library of Congress Control Number: 2014933084
Cataloging-in-Publication Data
Jackson, Dave, 1970-
 Philadelphia Phillies / by Dave Jackson.
  p. cm. -- (Inside MLB)
 Includes bibliographical references and index.
 ISBN 978-1-62403-480-0
 1. Philadelphia Phillies (Baseball team)--History--Juvenile literature. I. Title.
 GV875.P45J34 2015
 796.357'640974811--dc23
                                2014933084

TABLE OF CONTENTS

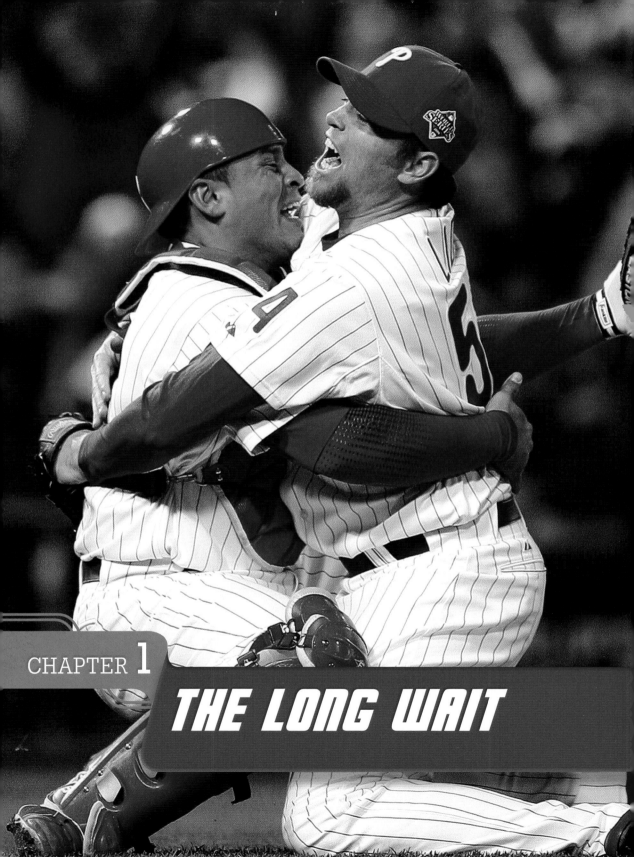

CHAPTER 1

THE LONG WAIT

Long-suffering Philadelphia fans were ready to celebrate. Their city had not won a professional sports title since 1983, 25 years earlier. But their baseball team, the Phillies, was one victory away from defeating the Tampa Bay Rays in the World Series.

As the teams took the field on October 27, 2008, for Game 5 of the Series, Philadelphia fans believed their team was only a few hours away from clinching the title and sending the city into a frenzy. And when the Phillies scored two runs in the first inning, the elusive championship seemed to be within reach.

But then it started to rain. A light rain began early in the game. It only got worse. By the sixth inning, Tampa Bay had tied the score at 2–2 and the field was so covered with puddles that the teams could not

Catcher Carlos Ruiz, *left*, and relief pitcher Brad Lidge celebrate after Philadelphia beat Tampa Bay 4–3 in Game 5 of the 2008 World Series. The Phillies earned their second Series title ever.

continue. Umpires stopped the game.

Phillies fans had reason to wonder: Was the rain a bad omen? Would the Phillies win? Or would the Rays come back and steal the Series away? Many players were frustrated that the game had even been started. Heavy rain had been forecast. For nearly two days, the rain continued, delaying the game further.

On October 29, the rain finally stopped and the game resumed. The Phillies immediately scored in the bottom of the sixth inning to go ahead 3–2. Tampa Bay answered with a run in the seventh. But the Phillies came right back when outfielder Pat Burrell, who had worn a Phillies uniform longer than any player at the time, doubled to lead off the bottom of the seventh. One out later, third baseman Pedro Feliz hit a run-scoring single to put the Phillies back on top.

As they entered the ninth inning with that slim 4–3 lead, the Phillies turned the game over to their best relief pitcher, Brad Lidge. Lidge had been perfect all year when the game was on the line. Every time Lidge had been brought in to save the game, he had succeeded—47 times in all. Now he needed one more save.

The Phillies' Jayson Werth, *left*, and Chase Utley congratulate each other after they scored during Game 5 of the 2008 World Series.

Lidge retired Evan Longoria on a pop-up but gave up a single to Dioner Navarro. Navarro left the game for pinch-runner Fernando Perez, who stole second base. Lidge then got a break when Ben Zobrist's line drive was caught by right fielder Jayson Werth.

Pinch-hitter Eric Hinske, a veteran hitter and a home-run

Home-Run Howard

Ryan Howard became the Phillies' first baseman midway through the 2005 season and hit well enough to be named the National League (NL) Rookie of the Year. The next year, he belted 58 home runs and won an even bigger honor—Most Valuable Player (MVP) of the league. Every year from 2006 to 2009, Howard hit at least 45 home runs. He had 31 in 2010 and 33 in 2011. No one in baseball history reached 200 career homers faster than Howard.

Philadelphia's Cole Hamels pitches during Game 5 of the 2008 World Series. The left-hander had a no-decision, but he pitched marvelously in that year's playoffs.

Playoff Ace

Cole Hamels was a promising left-handed pitching prospect when the Phillies called him up to the major leagues in 2006. He won nine games in 2006, 15 in 2007, and 14 more in 2008. But it was in the playoffs in 2008 that Hamels really fulfilled his promise. He started five games in the postseason, and the Phillies won all of them. Hamels went 4–0 and was named MVP of both the NL Championship Series (NLCS), in which the Phillies beat the Los Angeles Dodgers in five games, and the World Series.

threat, came to the plate. A single would likely tie the game. A home run might win it. Lidge quickly got two strikes on Hinske. Lidge then threw his best pitch, a slider that would drop sharply near the plate. Hinske waved his bat at it but missed. Strike three!

Lidge and catcher Carlos Ruiz jumped into each other's arms near the mound. The entire Phillies team soon joined

them in a joyous pile of cele-
bration. Lidge had completed
his perfect season. Philadelphia could finally claim
another championship, 25
years after the city's 76ers
won the National Basketball
Association (NBA) title.

And for just the second
time in their 125-year history,
the Phillies were the champi-
ons of baseball.

A PERFECT ADDITION

The Phillies were looking for a reliable pitcher out of the bullpen in 2008, so they took a chance on Brad Lidge. They sent three players to the Houston Astros in exchange for Lidge, who had saved 122 games from 2004 to 2007.

But after giving up a long home run to the St. Louis Cardinals' Albert Pujols in the 2005 playoffs, Lidge had struggled to regain the dominance that had earned him the nickname "Lights Out" Lidge. After joining the Phillies, he became Lights Out again. His 48-for-48 performance in save situations in 2008, including 7-for-7 in the postseason, marked the second time in baseball history that a pitcher had saved that many games in a season without a blown save.

Lidge was on the mound when the Phillies clinched the NL East Division in 2008 and again when they won each of their playoff series that year.

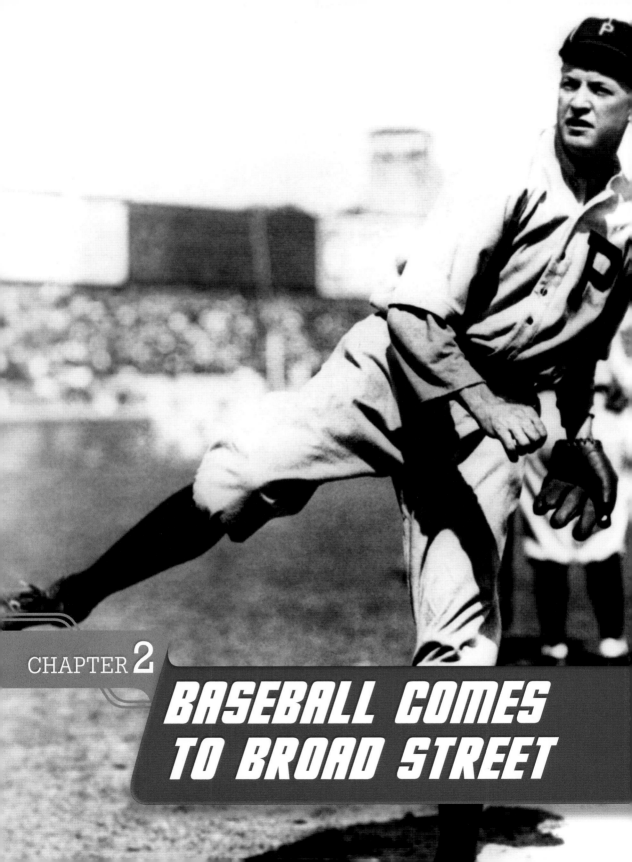

CHAPTER 2

BASEBALL COMES TO BROAD STREET

Since 1883, the Phillies franchise has called Philadelphia home. The team began play as a replacement team for the Worcester (Massachusetts) Ruby Legs of the NL. Two local men, Al Reach and John Rogers, became the team owners. They chose the name "Phillies" in honor of their city.

Though the Phillies did not win the NL pennant until 1915, their teams in the 1800s were generally competitive and featured several Hall of Famers. Their 1894 team included three outfielders—Ed Delahanty, Billy Hamilton, and Sam Thompson—who would all make the Baseball Hall of Fame. All three hit better than .400 that year. In 1896, Delahanty was the first of three Phillies players to hit four home runs in one game. Hamilton became one of the game's great base stealers. He finished with 914 stolen bases in his

Hall of Famer Grover Cleveland Alexander went 190–91 with a 2.18 ERA from 1911 to 1917 for the Phillies. He also pitched for the team in 1930.

career. Through 2013, this was the third-highest total in baseball history.

After playing their first four years in Recreation Park, the Phillies moved to Philadelphia Park in 1887. The park was built on the city's north side at Broad Street and Lehigh Avenue. That location became the Phillies' home for the next 51 years. The original Philadelphia Park was destroyed by fire in 1894. A new one was built on the same spot one year later. This park, which was later renamed Baker Bowl, was hailed as the best stadium in the nation.

The park also had an unusual playing field. Builders needed to fit the park into the space of just one city block. So while the center-field fence stood more than 400 feet from home plate, the right-field wall was just 280 feet away. This made for an inviting target for home-run hitters.

In 1899, the Phillies won 94 games. This set a team record that would stand for 77 years. The team included Delahanty and two other future Hall of Famers—second baseman Nap Lajoie and outfielder Elmer Flick. Delahanty led the NL in batting average, hits, and runs batted in (RBIs). But despite their success, the

The 1889 Phillies pose for a portrait. Sam Thompson, *front row center*, and Ed Delahanty, *third from left in the middle row*, would be enshrined in the Baseball Hall of Fame.

Phillies finished the season nine games behind first-place Brooklyn. They would have to wait another 16 years to win their first pennant.

The team began to fall when the NL was faced with a rival in 1901. The AL formed that year and began buying players away from the NL.

Before the Babe

Baseball was not a home-run hitter's game until Babe Ruth became a regular outfielder in 1919. Before Ruth, the sport's most prolific home-run hitter was the Phillies' Gavvy Cravath. He led the NL in home runs six times between 1913 and 1919. Through 2013, only three players had won more home-run titles than Cravath: Ruth (12 titles), Mike Schmidt (eight), and Ralph Kiner (seven).

The Phillies' Chuck Klein led the NL in home runs in 1929, 1931, 1932, and 1933. He hit at least 28 homers in all of those seasons.

Starting with a Bang

The quirky Baker Bowl was friendly to Phillies outfielder Chuck Klein. In his first full season with the team, in 1929, Klein hit 43 home runs. The left-handed hitter knew how to take advantage of the short right-field fence at the Phillies' home park. From 1929 to 1933, Klein averaged 36 home runs and 139 RBIs per season. In 1933, he won the Triple Crown by leading the NL in batting average, home runs, and RBIs.

Lajoie, Delahanty, and Flick all left the Phillies. All three would win batting titles once they joined the AL. Meanwhile, the Phillies struggled through most of the new century's first 10 years.

The Phillies' fortunes began to turn when rookie pitcher Grover Cleveland Alexander joined the team in 1911.

Alexander won 28 games in his rookie year. He would win 190 games in his seven years with the Phillies. In 1915, Alexander went 31–10 with a 1.22 earned-run average (ERA) in leading the Phillies to their first World Series. He won the first game against the Boston Red Sox. But the Phillies lost the next four games and fell in the Series.

The Phillies' success did not last. After trading Alexander to the Chicago Cubs after the 1917 season, they finished in last place 17 times between 1918 and 1948. It seemed that the team's destiny was to become the NL's doormat, until a scrappy group came along in 1950.

A BAD DEAL

The Phillies' infamous trade of pitcher Grover Cleveland Alexander to the Chicago Cubs in December 1917 started with a war.

When the United States entered World War I in 1917, the military drafted a number of major league players. Alexander was on the list, and the Phillies did not want to lose him to the draft. So they traded him instead. Alexander served a year in the military and missed most of the 1918 season. He resumed a Hall of Fame career the next year, winning 16 games in 1919 and 27 in 1920 with the Cubs. Alexander's 90 shutouts are an NL record.

What about the two players the Phillies received? Pitcher Mike Prendergast had a decent campaign in 1918 but was out of baseball after the next season. Catcher Pickles Dillhoefer managed just 11 at-bats in 1918 before the Phillies dealt him.

The Alexander trade was the worst in Phillies history.

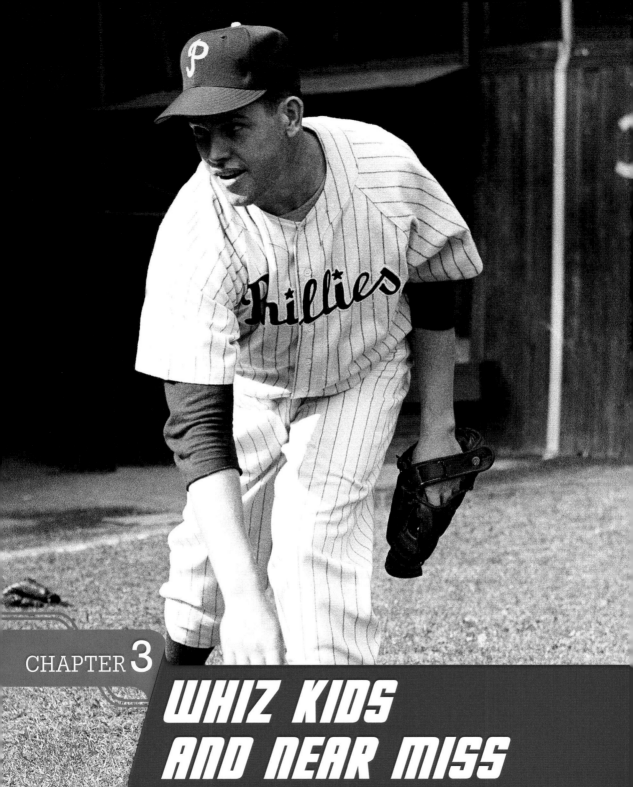

CHAPTER 3

WHIZ KIDS
AND NEAR MISS

The Phillies went 81–73 in 1949 for their first winning season in 17 years. But no one expected them to become contenders in 1950. The Phillies were the youngest team in baseball at the start of the season. A Florida sportswriter who saw the team play during spring training called them the "Whiz Kids."

The offense was led by speedy center fielder Richie Ashburn, who hit .303 and went on to the Hall of Fame, and Philadelphia native Del Ennis, an outfielder who batted .311 with 31 home runs and 126 RBIs. Relief pitcher Jim Konstanty went 16–7 with 22 saves and won the NL MVP Award. The Phillies' starting pitchers included right-hander Robin Roberts (20–11), a future Hall of Famer, and lefty Curt Simmons (17–8).

Philadelphia caught fire in July and August to take over first place. On September 20,

Phillies pitcher Robin Roberts is shown on October 3, 1950, preparing for the World Series against the Yankees. Philadelphia's "Whiz Kids" team surprised many baseball followers by reaching the Series that year.

RICHIE ASHBURN

Perhaps no Phillies player has been more of a fan favorite than Richie Ashburn.

The fleet center fielder from Tilden, Nebraska, was nicknamed "Whitey" for his light blond hair, which later turned white. He joined the team in 1948 and spent 12 seasons with the Phillies. He hit .300 or better eight times and won two NL batting titles. He also stole 199 bases and played terrific defense.

Ashburn's greatest play came on the final day of the 1950 season, when he threw out the Dodgers' Cal Abrams at home plate in the ninth inning. Had Abrams scored, the Dodgers would have won and forced a playoff for the pennant. The Phillies eventually won the game and clinched a spot in the World Series.

After he retired, Ashburn joined the Phillies' broadcast team in 1963 and called games until his death in 1997. Ashburn was inducted into the Baseball Hall of Fame in 1995.

the Phillies led the league by 7 1/2 games with only 11 to play. But their pitching staff began to fall apart. Simmons was called into military duty. Two other pitchers, Bubba Church and Bob Miller, were injured. The defending league champion Brooklyn Dodgers began to close the gap.

The Phillies lost eight of 10 games and held just a one-game lead over the Dodgers going into the season's final day. The teams played each other. They went to extra innings tied at 1–1. Then Philadelphia's Dick Sisler hit a three-run homer to put his team ahead. Roberts retired the Dodgers in the bottom of the 10th for a complete-game win that gave the Phillies their first pennant in 35 years.

The Phillies lost the 1950 World Series in four consecutive games to the New York

Left to right, outfielders Del Ennis, Richie Ashburn, and Dick Sisler pose in 1950. That year, those players helped the Phillies win their first pennant since 1915.

Yankees. Despite being such a young team, the Phillies never came close to winning the pennant again with those players. The team returned to its losing ways. Philadelphia hit rock bottom in 1961. The team went 47–107 and had a major league-record 23-game losing streak.

But young players such as Johnny Callison, Tony Taylor, and Tony Gonzalez were developing into stars. In 1964, two newcomers joined them. The Phillies traded with the Detroit Tigers for standout pitcher Jim Bunning. Also, young third baseman Richie Allen was

Third baseman Richie Allen is shown in 1964. Allen won the NL Rookie of the Year Award that year, but the Phillies faltered late in the season.

Father's Day Present

There were many reasons that Father's Day was special for Phillies pitcher Jim Bunning. He had seven children. But Father's Day on June 21, 1964, at Shea Stadium in New York was extra special. Bunning faced 27 Mets that day—and he retired them all. It was the first regular-season perfect game in 42 years and the first no-hitter by a Phillies pitcher in 58 years. Bunning struck out 10 batters, including the final one, Johnny Stephenson.

ready to play every day. Allen hit .318 with 29 home runs and Bunning went 19–8 as the Phillies again took a big lead into September.

This time the Phillies led by 6 1/2 games with only 12 games left. The team began printing World Series tickets for fans to buy. Once again, however, the Phillies fell apart in the season's final weeks.

Unlike in 1950, they were not able to recover. The Phillies lost 10 games in a row. The St. Louis Cardinals passed them to win the pennant by one game.

It was another frustrating finish. By the end of the 1960s, the Phillies were back to their losing ways. In 1969, the NL split into two six-team divisions. In their division, the Phillies finished fifth in 1969 and 1970 and sixth in 1971, 1972, and 1973.

The team had reasons for hope, however. The Phillies had a new home. They played their final game at old Connie Mack Stadium in 1970 and left North Philadelphia for South Philadelphia. Veterans Stadium, which like many other big-league ballparks of the era featured artificial turf, opened in 1971. Philadelphia had built up a strong farm system. As the 1970s started, many of those players would be ready for the major leagues. They would form the team's core during one of the most successful periods in Phillies history.

Hitting Machine

The 1960s were a decade largely dominated by major league pitchers, until the pitching mound was lowered in 1969 to take away some of their advantage. But Dick Allen was one of the best hitters of this era. Called "Richie" when he came to the majors, he had one of the best rookie seasons ever in 1964 and won the NL Rookie of the Year Award. In each of his first four years, he batted .302 or better with at least 25 doubles, 10 triples, and 20 home runs. After leaving the Phillies following the 1969 season, he went on to win the 1972 AL MVP Award with the Chicago White Sox before returning to the Phillies in 1975.

CHAPTER 4

PHINALLY

The Phillies finished their first three seasons at Veterans Stadium in last place. But they began to build around a young core of players that included shortstop Larry Bowa, outfielder Greg Luzinski, and catcher Bob Boone.

Before the 1972 season, the Phillies made an important trade. They acquired pitcher Steve Carlton from the St. Louis Cardinals. At the end of that season, they called up a young third baseman, Mike Schmidt.

By 1975, Schmidt and Luzinski had become a formidable home-run duo for the Phillies. The team jumped to third place in 1974 and second place in 1975. Meanwhile, more trades brought key players to the team. Reliever Tug McGraw, for example, was acquired from the New York Mets after the 1974 season.

Steve Carlton pitches in 1976. The Hall of Famer played for the Phillies from 1972 to 1986 and won four NL Cy Young Awards with the team.

Adding a Lefty

The Phillies' trade of pitcher Rick Wise to the St. Louis Cardinals for pitcher Steve Carlton in 1972 turned out to be their best. Carlton quickly became a fan favorite by winning a remarkable 27 games on a last-place team in 1972. He won the Cy Young Award that year and did so again in 1977, 1980, and 1982 for Philadelphia. The tall left-hander won 241 games for the Phillies in 15 seasons, and he pitched in the big leagues until 1988. He compiled a career record of 329–244 with 4,136 strikeouts. He entered the Baseball Hall of Fame in 1994.

In 1976, the Phillies took the final step. They won 101 games to capture the NL East Division title by nine games. The Cincinnati Reds swept the Phillies in three games in the NLCS. But Philadelphia had again laid a foundation for success with a young team.

Unlike 1950 and 1964, however, the Phillies maintained their success. The 1977 team also won 101 games and the division. And in 1978, the Phillies won their third straight division title. But in both 1977 and 1978, the Los Angeles Dodgers eliminated the Phillies in four games in the NLCS. It seemed as if Philadelphia was missing one key player to put it over the top.

After the 1978 season, the Phillies got that player. Baseball's premier free agent during that off-season was Pete Rose. He was a star on the Reds' back-to-back World Series championship teams in 1975 and 1976. The Reds were rebuilding and did not try to sign Rose. He chose the Phillies.

Though the Phillies fell to fourth place in 1979, they entered 1980 with a new manager, Dallas Green. He had taken over late in the 1979 campaign. There was a feeling that this would be the team's last chance at a championship.

Mike Schmidt, one of baseball's top power hitters ever, swings in the 1970s. Schmidt helped the Phillies reach the postseason four times between 1976 and 1980.

Schmidt had an MVP season. He blasted 48 home runs. Carlton finished 24–9 to win his third Cy Young Award. As the season came down to its final weekend, the Phillies were tied with the Montreal Expos for first place. The teams would play three games in Montreal.

Schmidt homered in each of the first two games, and the Phillies won both. His two-run homer in the 11th inning of the second game led to a 6–4 win for

MIKE SCHMIDT

Many fans have debates about the greatest players in their favorite team's history, but for Phillies fans there is a clear answer about who was the best. It was Mike Schmidt.

Schmidt is also perhaps the greatest third baseman in baseball history. His rookie season of 1973 was disappointing, as Schmidt batted just .196. But in 1974, he improved to .282 and led the NL in home runs with 36. Schmidt won eight NL home-run titles. Through 2013, only Babe Ruth led his league in home runs more times, with 12 titles.

Schmidt was not just an offensive player; he was also one of the top defensive players ever at his position. He won 10 Gold Glove Awards.

Schmidt won three NL MVP Awards, including one in the Phillies' title season of 1980, when he smashed a career-high 48 home runs. Schmidt retired in 1989 and was selected to the Baseball Hall of Fame in 1995.

the Phillies and their fourth division title in five years. Now they had to take the next step: win a playoff series.

The Phillies played the Houston Astros in the NLCS. Four of the five games went to extra innings in the thrilling series. The teams split the first two games in Philadelphia and went to Houston for the final three. The Astros took Game 3 by a score of 1–0, putting the Phillies one loss away from another near miss.

This time things were different. The Phillies came from behind to win 5–3 in Game 4 in 10 innings. In Game 5, Gary Maddox doubled home what proved to be the winning run in the 10th inning as the visiting Phillies won 8–7 for their first NL pennant in 30 years.

In the World Series, the Phillies met the Kansas City Royals. The Series featured

Tug McGraw reacts after he recorded the last out in Philadelphia's 4–1 win over Kansas City in Game 6 of the 1980 World Series. The Phillies earned their first Series title.

a matchup of MVP third basemen, Schmidt and the Royals' George Brett. The crucial game was Game 5. The Phillies scored two runs in the top of the ninth to edge out the Royals 4–3. In Game 6, Schmidt hit an early two-run single, Carlton went seven strong innings, and McGraw pitched out of a bases-loaded jam in the ninth. He struck out Willie Wilson for the final out of the 4–1 victory. McGraw's Phillies teammates mobbed him on the mound.

Fans at Veterans Stadium rejoiced. After 97 years of existence, the Phillies franchise finally had a championship.

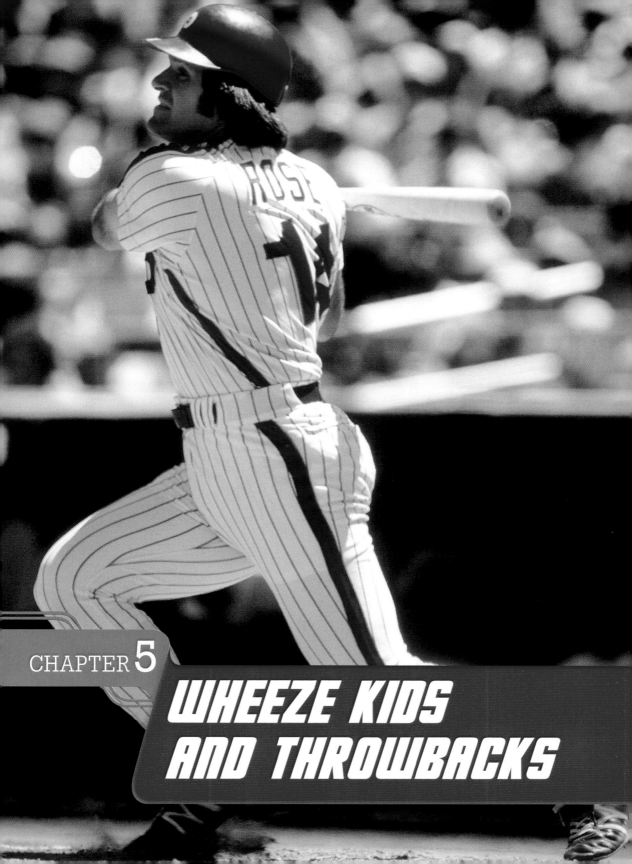

CHAPTER 5

WHEEZE KIDS AND THROWBACKS

On the heels of their first World Series championship, the Phillies started out the 1981 season well. But on June 12, major league players went on strike in their effort to get a new contract. No more games were played until August.

Because of the long break, Major League Baseball split the season in half and staged an extra round of playoffs in each division. The Phillies had won the NL East's first half, so they were automatically in the postseason. But the strike cost the team its edge. Philadelphia went just 25–27 in the second half and lost to the Montreal Expos three games to two in the special division playoff series.

Two players who were not affected by the strike were Pete Rose and Mike Schmidt. Rose had to wait two months to break Stan Musial's NL record

Pete Rose swings in the early 1980s. Rose, who would later become baseball's all-time hits leader, played for Philadelphia from 1979 to 1983.

for career hits. He tied Musial in the last game before the strike but struck out in his final three at-bats in that game. On August 10, he got his record-breaking hit. Rose finished the season hitting .325 for his 15th season of batting .300 or better. Schmidt won his second consecutive NL MVP honor with a .316 average, 31 homers, and 91 RBIs.

Two years later, Rose and Schmidt were back in the World Series with the Phillies. Pitcher John Denny won 19 games and

the Cy Young Award in 1983 as the Phillies won their fifth division title in eight years. They beat an old nemesis, the Los Angeles Dodgers, in the NLCS but lost the World Series in five games to the Baltimore Orioles.

Because so many of the Phillies' regulars were older than 30, including Rose and his former Cincinnati Reds teammates Joe Morgan and Tony Perez, the team was called the "Wheeze Kids." And 1983 would be their last hurrah. Rose, Morgan, Perez, and outfielder Gary Matthews would all leave the team after the 1983 season. The Phillies began to rebuild.

In the next nine seasons, the Phillies would finish above .500 only once. That came in 1986, when Schmidt won his third MVP Award. But even then the Phillies ended up 21 1/2 games behind the first-place New York Mets.

Gary Matthews receives congratulations from Phillies teammate Tony Perez after Matthews homered in the 1983 World Series. Philadelphia fell in five games to Baltimore.

The Phillies finished in last place in 1988, 1989, and 1992. They again appeared to be returning to their foundation of losing baseball. But in 1993, a surprising group of hard-nosed Phillies captured Philadelphia's hearts. Led by center fielder Lenny Dykstra, catcher Darren Daulton, and first baseman John Kruk, the Phillies built an 11 1/2-game lead in the division.

The 1993 Phillies were very popular in Philadelphia. The team had several characters. The oversized Kruk described himself: "I'm not a

Number 500

Mike Schmidt's 500th home run was a memorable one. He hit a three-run homer off the Pittsburgh Pirates' Don Robinson with two outs in the ninth inning on April 18, 1987, to give the Phillies an 8–6 win. Schmidt finished his career with 548 home runs, all of them in a Phillies uniform. That total was good for seventh place on baseball's all-time list at the time of his retirement.

model. I don't get paid to look good." Dykstra played with a reckless style that usually left his uniform covered with dirt. Reliever Mitch Williams made fans nervous by working into and out of trouble nearly every time he took the mound.

True to their history, though, that year's Phillies did not make things easy on their fans. Their lead dwindled to four games in September. But they clinched the division on September 28 after leading for all but one day of the season.

In the NLCS, the Phillies surprised the favored Atlanta Braves by winning in six games. Then they faced the defending champion Toronto Blue Jays in the World Series. After splitting the first two games in Toronto, the Phillies lost the next two games at home. The second of those losses, a 15–14 slugfest in which the Phillies blew a late five-run lead, looked as if it would break the team's back.

But Curt Schilling's shutout in Game 5 lifted Philadelphia to a 2–0 win and sent the series back to Toronto. In Game 6, the Phillies came back from a 5–1 deficit to take a 6–5 lead entering the ninth. Williams tried to finish the game and force a deciding seventh game. Williams saved 43 games during the season. But his struggles with control earned him the nickname "Wild Thing." Williams walked leadoff hitter

John Kruk, *right*, celebrates with Phillies teammates after he scored during Game 1 of the 1993 World Series. Philadelphia lost the Series in six games to Toronto.

Rickey Henderson and put two men on base with one out when Jays cleanup hitter Joe Carter came to the plate.

Williams tried to throw a fastball by Carter. But Carter drove the pitch over the left-field wall for a three-run homer and an 8–6 victory that ended the Series. The Phillies had fallen short of their goal. But their rise from nowhere and their toughness made them one of their city's most beloved sports teams.

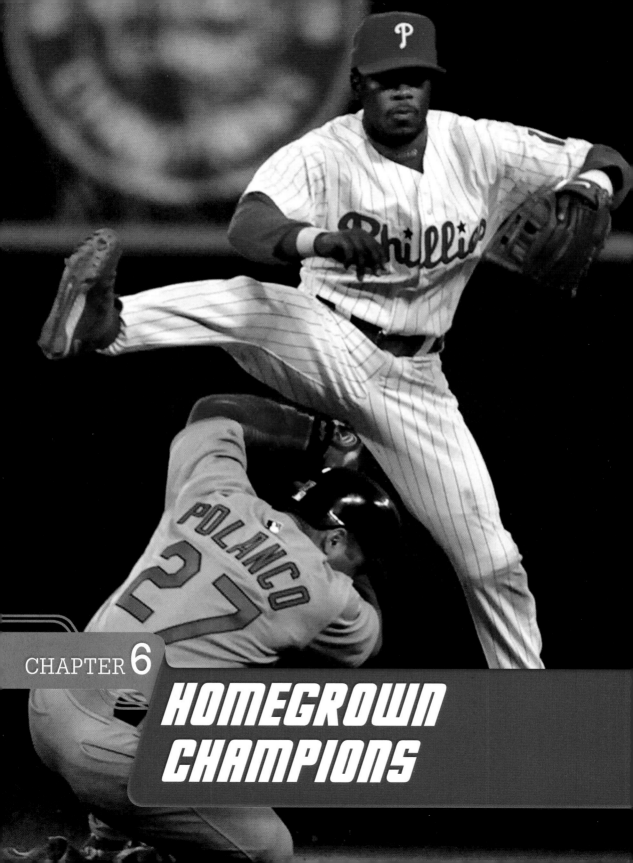

CHAPTER 6

HOMEGROWN
CHAMPIONS

After the 1993 season, the Phillies yet again appeared to have been one-year wonders. The 1994 season ended when players again went on strike. This time the World Series was canceled for the first time ever. Even had it been played, the Phillies probably would not have been in it. They finished 54–61 and never had a winning record for the rest of the decade.

But they began 2001 with a new manager and a new outlook. Larry Bowa brought the same fiery style that had made him a key player on the 1980 World Series team. Just like 1993, the Phillies started the season well and maintained first place in the NL East until midsummer. Then, the Atlanta Braves caught up with them.

In the end, the Braves held off the Phillies by two games. But the Phillies were starting

Rookie shortstop Jimmy Rollins jumps over the Cardinals' Placido Polanco in 2001. Rollins would be a key Phillies player for years to come.

BANKING ON SUCCESS

After 33 seasons in functional but sterile Veterans Stadium, the Phillies moved into Citizens Bank Park in April 2004.

"The Bank," as it is often called, joined the trend of recent baseball stadiums that combined modern conveniences with the look and feel of old-time ballparks. Traces of Phillies history can be seen throughout the park. Statues of Phillies greats Mike Schmidt, Steve Carlton, Robin Roberts, and Richie Ashburn stand in and around the park, with the pedestrian walkway beyond the outfield called Ashburn Alley. Bull's BBQ, managed by Phillies great Greg Luzinski, serves up food every game day.

More than 3.6 million fans came to the park in 2009, a team attendance record. In 2010, even more fans came through the gates.

to build a new core of players around third baseman Scott Rolen and outfielder Bobby Abreu. The 2001 team also featured rookie shortstop Jimmy Rollins, who batted .274 and stole 46 bases, and second-year outfielder Pat Burrell, who hit 27 home runs. Both would become team cornerstones for the entire decade. They would help lead the Phillies back to the playoffs.

Second baseman Chase Utley, first baseman Ryan Howard, and pitchers Brett Myers and Cole Hamels would eventually join Rollins and Burrell. Those players had all been drafted and developed in the team's farm system.

Every year from 2003 to 2006, the Phillies won at least 85 games. But they kept falling just short of the playoffs. They were in the postseason hunt during the season's final

Philadelphia's Ryan Howard follows through after homering in 2006. Howard led the majors with 58 home runs and 149 RBIs that year and was named NL MVP.

week in 2003, 2005, and 2006, only to miss out. In 2007, they were headed for another near miss when a 12–0 loss to the Colorado Rockies put them seven games behind the first-place New York Mets with 17 games to play.

But the Phillies went to New York and swept the Mets in three games on the way to winning 12 of 16 games. Meanwhile, the Mets lost 11 of 16 games. This left the two teams tied going into the final day of the season. After watching the

Cliff Lee pitches during Game 1 of the 2009 World Series. Lee earned two wins in the Series, but the defending champion Phillies fell in six games to the Yankees.

Florida Marlins grab an early lead against the host Mets, the Phillies took the field and beat the visiting Washington Nationals 6–1. When the Marlins finished off the Mets, the Phillies had improbably won the NL East.

Though Philadelphia would lose its first-round playoff series to Colorado in three straight games, the team had finally had a taste of success. In 2008, they again rallied from a September deficit to win the NL East. This time, they defeated the Milwaukee Brewers in the first round of the playoffs. They then beat the Los Angeles Dodgers in the NLCS. The magical season ended when they defeated the Tampa Bay Rays for their first world championship in 28 years.

In 2009, the Phillies led the division from May 30 until the end of the season. Howard, Utley, and outfielders Jayson Werth and Raul Ibanez became the 12th group of four teammates to each hit 30 home runs in a season. Cliff Lee and Pedro Martinez, both acquired that season, stabilized the pitching.

The Phillies made it back to the World Series after beating the Rockies and the Dodgers in the playoffs. But there would be no repeat championship. Despite two wins by Lee and five home runs by Utley, the Phillies lost to the powerful New York Yankees in six games.

For the 2010 season, the Phillies kept nearly all of their key offensive players. They also added Roy Halladay in an off-season trade for three prospects. Halladay finished 21–10 with a 2.44 ERA. In essence, he replaced Lee, whom the Phillies traded before the season to the Seattle Mariners for three prospects. With Halladay's help, the Phillies won a fourth consecutive

Hometown Hero

Life came full circle for Phillies pitcher Jamie Moyer in 2008. Moyer grew up outside Philadelphia as a fan of the team, and he skipped school the day the 1980 Phillies rode down Broad Street in a parade to celebrate their World Series win. Twenty-eight years later, Moyer was back on Broad Street as a member of the Phillies' second World Series championship team. His 16 wins led the Phillies during the regular season. "In our own small way, we've been able to bring baseball back to Philadelphia, to bring the Phillies back on the map," Moyer said.

Roy Halladay, *left*, celebrates with catcher Carlos Ruiz after throwing the second postseason no-hitter in baseball history. The gem lifted the Phillies to a 4–0 win over the Reds in Game 1 of the 2010 NLDS.

End of an Era

Harry Kalas joined the Phillies' broadcasting team in 1971. For the next 38 years, he was beloved by fans for his signature calls, such as, "That ball is outta here!" on a home run. In the spring of 2009, prior to a Phillies game in Washington DC, Kalas collapsed and died. The team wore "HK" uniform patches throughout 2009 in Kalas's honor.

NL East crown. They swept the Cincinnati Reds in three games in the NLCS. In Game 1, Halladay struck out eight and walked just one while pitching the second postseason no-hitter in baseball history. However, the Phillies were denied a third straight trip to the World

Series when the San Francisco Giants upset them in the NLCS, going on to win the World Series.

The Phillies played strong in 2011. They finished with 102 wins, their best record ever. Yet, the St. Louis Cardinals defeated them in the NLDS.

In 2012, the Phillies struggled. Utley, Howard, and Halladay suffered injuries. The team finished 81–81, missing the postseason for the first time since 2006.

The Phillies fell further behind in 2013, finishing the season 73–89. Mid-season, they got a new manager, Ryne Sandberg. In December, Halladay announced his retirement. Yet, the team appeared poised and ready for more success in the future.

HALLADAY'S BIG YEAR

In his first season in a Philadelphia uniform, ace right-hander Roy Halladay had an amazing year.

The veteran won an NL-high 21 games and the league's Cy Young Award. But that did not tell his whole story in 2010. On May 29, he pitched the 20th perfect game in big-league history, lifting Philadelphia to a 1–0 road victory over the Florida Marlins. Halladay did not allow a base runner by any means, and he struck out 11.

Halladay then topped that achievement by pitching a no-hitter on October 6 in the Phillies' 4–0 win over the visiting Cincinnati Reds in Game 1 of the NLDS. It was Halladay's first postseason appearance. The no-hitter was just the second in major league playoff history. The only previous postseason no-hitter was Don Larsen's perfect game for the New York Yankees against the Brooklyn Dodgers in Game 5 of the 1956 World Series.

TIMELINE

1883	The Philadelphia Phillies are formed when the NL's Worcester (Massachusetts) Ruby Legs go out of business.
1915	The Phillies reach their first World Series but fall in five games to the Boston Red Sox.
1917	Fearful of losing pitcher Grover Cleveland Alexander to the military draft, the Phillies trade him to the Chicago Cubs in December. Philadelphia goes on to finish in last place 17 times in the next 31 seasons.
1950	The Phillies reach their second World Series after a dramatic win on the final day of the season against the Brooklyn Dodgers. But the "Whiz Kids" are swept by the New York Yankees in the Series.
1964	Jim Bunning pitches the first perfect game in Phillies history, retiring all 27 batters and leading Philadelphia to a 6–0 victory over the host New York Mets on June 21.
1964	With World Series tickets already printed, the Phillies lose 10 games in a row near the end of the season and fail to win the pennant. The team had led the division by 6 1/2 games with only 12 games remaining.
1972	Pitcher Steve Carlton and third baseman Mike Schmidt play their first games as Phillies. Carlton, acquired from the St. Louis Cardinals before the season, goes 27–10 and wins the first of his four NL Cy Young Awards.
1976	The Phillies win their first of three consecutive NL East Division titles. All three times, they lose in the NLCS.

1980	The Phillies win their first World Series. They beat the Kansas City Royals in six games. Tug McGraw strikes out the Royals' Willie Wilson for the last out on October 21, securing the title for the Phillies.
1983	The Phillies return to the World Series but lose in five games to the Baltimore Orioles.
1993	The Phillies win the NL pennant. After beating the Atlanta Braves in the NLCS, the team loses the World Series to the Toronto Blue Jays.
2008	The Phillies win the NL East crown a second straight time, then beat the Milwaukee Brewers and the Los Angeles Dodgers in the first two rounds of the playoffs to reach the World Series. Brad Lidge strikes out the Tampa Bay Rays' Eric Hinske in Game 5 to wrap up a 4–3 home win for Philadelphia. The Phillies earn their second Series title.
2009	Following their third straight division championship, the Phillies return to the World Series but lose in six games to the New York Yankees.
2010	The Phillies win a fourth straight NL East championship. Roy Halladay pitches the 20th perfect game in baseball history and the second in Phillies history on May 29. He then pitches the second postseason no-hitter in MLB history on October 6 in Game 1 of the NLDS.
2011	The Phillies finish the regular season with 102 wins. This is the team's best record ever.
2013	The Phillies get a new manager, Ryne Sandberg. Sandberg was previously the team's third base coach and infield instructor.

QUICK STATS

FRANCHISE HISTORY
1883–

WORLD SERIES
(wins in bold)

1915, 1950, **1980**, 1983, 1993, **2008**, 2009

NL CHAMPIONSHIP SERIES
(1969–)

1976, 1977, 1978, 1980, 1983, 1993, 2008, 2009, 2010

KEY PLAYERS
(position[s]; seasons with team)

Grover Cleveland Alexander (SP; 1911–17, 1930)
Dick Allen (3B/1B; 1963–69, 1975–76)
Richie Ashburn (OF; 1948–59)

Jim Bunning (SP; 1964–67, 1970–71)
Steve Carlton (SP; 1972–86)
Ed Delahanty (OF; 1888–89, 1891–1901)
Ryan Howard (1B; 2004–)
Chuck Klein (OF; 1928–33, 1936–39, 1940–44)
Greg Luzinski (OF; 1970–80)
Robin Roberts (SP; 1948–61)
Jimmy Rollins (SS; 2000–)
Mike Schmidt (3B/1B; 1972–89)
Chase Utley (2B; 2003–)

KEY MANAGERS

Dallas Green (1979–81): 169–130; 9–7 (postseason)
Charlie Manuel (2005–2013): 544–428; 25–16 (postseason)

HOME PARKS

Recreation Park (1883–86)
Philadelphia Baseball Grounds/ Baker Bowl (1887–1938)
Shibe Park/Connie Mack Stadium (1938–70)
Veterans Stadium (1971–2003)
Citizens Bank Park (2004–)

* All statistics through 2013 season

QUOTES AND ANECDOTES

The Phillies' long history of losing resulted in them becoming the first franchise in sports to record 10,000 losses. Their 10,000th loss ironically came during 2007, when they began a string of division championship seasons. On July 15 of that year, the visiting St. Louis Cardinals beat the Phillies 10–2. "I don't know much about 10,000 losses," Philadelphia manager Charlie Manuel said. "I try to concentrate on the wins."

Before the 2007 season, Jimmy Rollins told reporters that the Phillies were "the team to beat" in the NL East. After Philadelphia had finished 12 games behind the New York Mets in 2006, many people ignored Rollins's comments. But the Phillies' shortstop backed up his talk by hitting .296 with 30 home runs and 41 stolen bases. He won the NL MVP Award, and the Phillies won the division title he had predicted.

The Phillies are the only team to have three different players hit four home runs in a game, and all three players are in the Hall of Fame. Ed Delahanty was the first to do so, hitting four homers on July 13, 1896, in a 9–8 loss to the host Chicago Colts. Chuck Klein hit four on July 10, 1936, as the visiting Phillies beat the Pittsburgh Pirates 9–6. Mike Schmidt became the third Phillies player to blast four homers when he achieved the feat in Philadelphia's wild 18–16 win over the host Chicago Cubs on April 17, 1976. Through 2013, 16 big-league players overall had hit four homers in a game, and five of those players were in the Hall of Fame. The Hall of Famers were the three Phillies players, plus Lou Gehrig and Willie Mays.

GLOSSARY

ace

A team's best starting pitcher.

acquire

To add a player, usually through the draft, free agency, or a trade.

cornerstone

A basic element of something, such as a player whom a team needs to win.

endear

To become loved or admired.

farm system

A big-league club's teams in the minor leagues, where players are developed for the majors.

franchise

An entire sports organization, including the players, coaches, and staff.

infamous

Having a negative reputation.

omen

A sign of something that will happen in the future, often something negative.

pennant

A flag. In baseball, it symbolizes that a team has won its league championship.

prolific

Very productive or successful.

prospect

A young player, usually one who has little major league experience.

sterile

Lacking unique or interesting qualities.

veteran

An individual with great experience in a particular endeavor.

FOR MORE INFORMATION

Further Reading

Stark, Jayson. *Worth the Wait: Tales of the 2008 Phillies.* Chicago: Triumph Books, 2009.

Westcott, Rich. *Philadelphia Phillies Past & Present.* Minneapolis: MVP Books, 2010.

Zolecki, Todd. *The Good, the Bad & the Ugly: Heart-Pounding, Jaw-Dropping, and Gut-Wrenching Moments from Philadelphia Phillies History.* Chicago: Triumph Books, 2010.

Web Links

To learn more about Inside MLB, visit **booklinks.abdopublishing.com**. These links are routinely monitored and updated to provide the most current information available.

Places to Visit

Bright House Field
601 Old Coachman Road
Clearwater, FL 33765
727-467-4457
Bright House Field has been the Phillies' spring-training ballpark since 2004.

Citizens Bank Park
One Citizens Bank Way
Philadelphia, PA 19148
215-463-1000
www.citizensbank.com/ballpark
This has been the Phillies' home field since 2004. The team plays 81 regular-season games here each year.

National Baseball Hall of Fame and Museum
25 Main Street
Cooperstown, NY 13326
888-425-5663
www.baseballhall.org
This hall of fame and museum highlights the greatest players and moments in the history of baseball. Many former Phillies players—including Richie Ashburn, Jim Bunning, Steve Carlton, Chuck Klein, Robin Roberts, and Mike Schmidt—have been enshrined here.

INDEX

About the Author

Dave Jackson is a freelance writer and former sportswriter with the *Star Tribune* and the Associated Press in Minneapolis, Minnesota. Since 1997, he has worked in corporate communications, helping large companies improve their communications with key stakeholders. He and his wife live in Dallas, Texas.